Soul of C

Soul of Cancers

Moonsoulchild

Soul of Cancers

Soul of Cancers

Copyright © 2021 Sara Sheehan
All Rights Reserved
ISBN: 9798771345222

Soul of Cancers

Soul of Cancers

Everything you see within these pages is from my experiences. I took those experiences and put them into words. This collection is for all Cancer placements but can relate to others who are not cancers. It just gets deeper for us Cancers. We're all different, so be mindful you may not relate to it all, or you may.

I hope you enjoy the read!

Soul of Cancers

Soul of Cancers

Cancer
June 21 – July 22

Symbol: The Crab
Element: Water
Ruling Planet: The Moon

Cancer, the **Moonchild**, is compassionate, loving, and deeply sensitive. We often hide in our shells because we find comfort in our *comfort* zone. We're protective and make sure our loved ones are safe and know they're loved. We can be *shy* but outgoing, especially when we find comfort in you. We're probably the most devoted to connections we behold, whether it's family, friendships or romantically, we strive to be the best partner in any connection because we love deeply and never wish to hurt anyone. We tend to feel everything deeply and we become overly *sensitive* and highly *moody* sometimes because it's difficult to balance our emotions. We love forever. We're someone who remembers everything, especially when it's someone close to us. We're loyal, sentimental, and affectionate. We're dedicated to being our best self and the best for our loved ones.

Soul of Cancers

Name: Moonsoulchild (Sara)

Cancer placement: Sun

Birthday: June 27, 1993

(Fill in the blanks)

Name:

Cancer placement:

Birthday:

Soul of Cancers

Describe yourself in 5 words

1. Loving
2. Empath
3. Intuitive
4. Creative
5. Imperfect

(fill in the blanks)

1.
2.
3.
4.
5.

Soul of Cancers

My **Toxic** Trait:

Ghosting when I felt there was nothing left to do or say. When I felt my absence wouldn't be missed. I adapted this to every situation when it became comforting. I chose to ghost when I was afraid to hurt someone when I didn't have it in me to communicate. I chose to push away people purposely because I thought I was preventing myself from getting hurt first, I ended up hurting myself more.

Soul of Cancers

What's Your **Toxic** Trait?

Soul of Cancers

Bad Traits You Have
(circle yours)

Ghosting

Being too forgiving

Pretending not to care

Vindictive

Self-pitying

Overthinking

Manipulation

Pushing people away

Ignoring red flags

Savior complex

Moody

Insecurity

Soul of Cancers

Good Traits You Have
(circle yours)

Loyal

Protective

Intuitive

Caring

Sensitive

Empath

Charming

Humorous

Creative

A huge heart

Soul of Cancers

Section One:

"Being a Cancer"

Soul of Cancers

A huge heart you won't forget.
Overly caring, emotional, and vulnerable.
My loyalty runs deep but don't cross me.
I've brought pain too.
Spiritually connected.
Intuition is my first language.
A love language unmatched.
A best friend you'll ever have.

I'm a **Cancer**.

Soul of Cancers

No one will love you more than a **Cancer**, but don't get it twisted, we know when to let go. We know when it's no longer healthy and completely toxic to our being.

Don't ever take our love for granted.

Soul of Cancers

Cancers are the best lovers, friends, and souls you'll ever meet. Our love runs deep, you'll feel it and you won't ever feel overlooked or unappreciated. Our loyalty is unmatched, we'll always look out for you and be good to you. Just don't betray us, we're also good at never looking back.

Soul of Cancers

Cancers are always misunderstood because our love language is unmatched. We've been taken for granted, manipulated, and used because of our vulnerability. Our love is always wanted but not always cherished. We're overlooked but always the ones to blame when it's time to let go.

Soul of Cancers

Being a **Cancer** feels like carrying the emotions of everyone you love on your shoulders. A therapist. An empath. A great friend. Sometimes it can get overwhelming, we tend to put the needs of everyone before our own.

Soul of Cancers

I'm a **Cancer**,

I remember energy and vibes. I'm an observer, I pay attention to detail. I remember everything about someone I love. I don't take what they say or do lightly, they deserve to have all of me, and I mean that without taking away from myself to do so.

Soul of Cancers

Being a **Cancer**,

We're deeply introverted, we crave alone time. We crave peace of mind. Our shell is our safe place.

Soul of Cancers

I'm a **Cancer**, which means I can read your energy before you approach me.

Soul of Cancers

I'm a **Cancer**, which means give me my space when I ask for it. My mouth tends to speak out of line when I'm hurt.

Soul of Cancers

I'm a **Cancer**,

People treat us like we're hard to love
because the capacity of love we have to give
is always more than what's reciprocated.
We're treated like our emotional being is
too intense to ever be matched.

Soul of Cancers

Cancers have this reputation of not being able to let go because we're so driven by the past and the comfort of the good that once was. The best thing for us is to let go when we're unwanted, our love is too worthy to be wasted.

Soul of Cancers

I'm a **Cancer**, I'll love you forever but that doesn't mean you need to be in my life for me to do so. When I let you go I don't plan on coming back.

Soul of Cancers

If you got a **Cancer**, you got a REAL one.

Soul of Cancers

One thing about us **Cancers**,

we're going to love you even when it hurts, that's our loyalty.

Soul of Cancers

Cancers,

You need to let go of:

1. The past
2. Your savior complex
3. Your unrequited love
4. The love that isn't healthy
5. The version of you that you don't think is good enough

Soul of Cancers

Cancers,

What do you need to let go of?

1.

2.

3.

4.

5.

Soul of Cancers

Cancers,

Don't ever stop:

1. Following your intuition
2. Being emotionally in tune
3. Being vulnerable
4. Crying
5. Giving love
6. Being the best version of yourself

Soul of Cancers

Cancers,

What are 5 things you'll never stop?

1.

2.

3.

4.

5.

Soul of Cancers

Us **Cancers** are known for being too sensitive, too emotional, and a cry baby. People overlook us because they're afraid of how deep our love goes. They're afraid they won't ever love us as we deserve, so they treat us like we're too much.

Soul of Cancers

I'm a **Cancer**, mood swings are usually a deal-breaker when it comes to anyone. No one can handle my emotions.

Soul of Cancers

Us **Cancers** are used to being outcasts. We never seem to fit in because we're never down with the hype. We live in our world, in our shell, introverted without care to fit in.

Soul of Cancers

We're **Cancers**, people either love us deeply or hate us intensely. Either way, we're living rent-free in minds, hearts, and souls. We're unforgettable.

Soul of Cancers

Crying is a form of therapy.

Sincerely,
A **Cancer**.

Soul of Cancers

Being a **Cancer** sometimes means disappearing into your shell until you feel like being social and you again.

Soul of Cancers

No one will ever love you like a **Cancer**, how they nurture you and always seem to find the best in you and bring it out. They love to the deepest of their core, even when it hurts, their love is rare and will always be remembered.

Soul of Cancers

Us **Cancers** aren't perfect, we make mistakes too, but that doesn't mean we're not worthy of good and love.

Soul of Cancers

Us **Cancers** took it personally when you decided to hurt us with a lie when you could have hurt them with the truth.

Soul of Cancers

I'm a **Cancer**, I either express way too much and pour my heart out to you, or I'm hidden away in my shell because I feel you don't care to hear me out.

Soul of Cancers

People love to hate us **Cancers**, they love to change the narrative and make us look like we're emotionally unstable to be with, except they're wrong, they never had what it took to understand us. We shouldn't need to apologize to anyone who wasn't ready for our love.

Soul of Cancers

We're not someone who opens up to anyone we're not comfortable around, not everyone can break through this shell, it's tough. Energy is important to us.

Sincerely,
A **Cancer**.

Soul of Cancers

I think people underestimate **Cancer's** ability to see through people. I don't think they understand we already read your energy, there's no need for you to top it off with a lie. This is why we're introverted; we have no time for fake company, we're tired of being misled.

Soul of Cancers

I'm a **Cancer**, I'm bad at disguising how I feel. I can't fake it. I don't ever want someone I love to question my loyalty.

Soul of Cancers

I'm a **Cancer**, I may act like I don't know but I'm way ahead of you. I'm waiting to see if you tell me first.

Soul of Cancers

I love raw vulnerability at best. I love when someone is open with me because they trust me, not because I broke down their wall. Someone who feels my energy and knows my intentions without a word. It's me, I'm a **Cancer**.

Soul of Cancers

You hurt a **Cancer** and we either try to save the connection, give a dozen second chances, or ghost you writing you out of our existence. Don't test how deep our love goes for you.

Soul of Cancers

Us **Cancers** are deeply affectionate. One of our biggest love languages is showing love through body language, but only if we trust you, not everyone gets that from us.

Soul of Cancers

My detective skills are always accurate. I find everything out. I can read energy before words are spoken. There's no point in lying to me, I'm always a step ahead, my intuition got me.

Sincerely,
A **Cancer**.

Soul of Cancers

Someone convinced me to close myself off once, to let my vulnerable self go and use my heartless. It ended up benefiting me at the end when I got rid of them without hurting myself too. I was lost but found my way through. A **Cancer** never forgets what it's like to feel.

Soul of Cancers

I dwell on the past often. I think about "what if" and almost convince myself it did happen. I overthink and make a bigger mess of what is. I'm a **Cancer**, I can't help it. I always feel the need to save everything.

Soul of Cancers

Cancers protect their feelings by pushing you away and acting like they don't care.

Soul of Cancers

I'm a **Cancer**, I either give you too many second chances or walk away and never look back. There's no in-between.

Soul of Cancers

I'm a **Cancer**, I value friendships and connections. I'll keep your darkest and deepest secrets and never use them against you. My level of loyalty is unmatched.

Soul of Cancers

I move differently, if I find someone acting funny, there's no question, I'll remove myself from their life. I don't have time to fight for a spot I'm not entitled to. I don't have the energy to fight to stay where I'm no longer wanted.

Sincerely,
A **Cancer**.

Soul of Cancers

Cancers, you have a heart so big and a soul so gentle, you should never be convinced you're hard to love.

Soul of Cancers

I'm a **Cancer**, I tend to push people away when I'm afraid to get hurt. I push people away sometimes to see if they love me enough to fight for me.

Soul of Cancers

Us **Cancers** crave our alone time just as much as we crave the presence of someone we love and the security they bring.

Soul of Cancers

I've pushed people away when I was afraid to get hurt, I ended up hurting myself instead.

Sincerely,
A **Cancer**.

Soul of Cancers

I'm a **Cancer**, I don't like confrontation or drama, but please know, if it involves something or someone, I'm passionate about, I will always show up.

Soul of Cancers

A **Cancer** doesn't become heartless, we become guarded.

Soul of Cancers

As someone emotionally in tune, we **Cancers** sometimes hide them too. We build walls where we were once broken. We make it hard for anyone to get through. It's like we take a chance and get broken, then take two steps back.

Soul of Cancers

I'm someone who holds a connection close, who doesn't open to anyone. If you don't come with a beautiful soul and a passionate heart, I don't want you around me. I don't have what it takes, anymore, to keep letting tainted love ruin me.

Sincerely,
A **Cancer**.

Soul of Cancers

Everyone will go around saying a **Cancer** hurt them and they're the worst but refuse to tell the story of how they pushed us to do so.

Soul of Cancers

Emotional and vulnerable, two traits I was never accepted for. I was always told to "dim" down my emotions, that my love was too intense. It was too much, but they also wanted my love. I've always been real; some weren't ready for my love.

Sincerely,
A **Cancer**.

Soul of Cancers

Half the time we're not truly introverted, we just reserve our energy for genuine souls. Not everyone gets to share that rare connection, let alone get close.

Sincerely,
A **Cancer**.

Soul of Cancers

Us **Cancers** can be emotionally manipulative when it comes to needing that security within any connection. We use our love as a weapon, believing our unconditional love can keep anyone, not knowing we deserve more.

Soul of Cancers

If the moon is out, I'm probably in my feels.
Don't take it personally.

Sincerely,
A **Cancer**.

Soul of Cancers

There's no such thing as a perfect person, we **Cancers** don't strive to be. We strive to be understood in a world that sees us as these overly sensitive people. We're always misunderstood. We live with years old trauma that we never let free; we're always striving to be free.

Soul of Cancers

Us **Cancers** feel everything so deeply, it's impossible for us to not feel a thing. We're ruled by the moon, with so many emotions. We don't ever want to be cold-hearted; we just want to be loved.

Soul of Cancers

I'm a **Cancer**, I always try to find the best in everyone. I always try and bring the good out of them, even if it hurts me.

Soul of Cancers

I'm a **Cancer**, a sucker for love, and a hopeless romantic. Our emotional being is intense, like our love, but it's never intended to hurt you. If we hurt someone we love, we hurt too.

Soul of Cancers

We may be overly emotional **Cancers**, but that doesn't mean we're overly forgiving. When we're over you, over the pain, over the constant toxicity. You're completely gone from our hearts but know the pain will always be remembered.

Soul of Cancers

I feel like sometimes people get it twisted and assume just because we're overly emotional doesn't mean we can't leave you behind. Us **Cancers** are great at detaching old connections when we're no longer romanticizing the past and realize it's only breaking us.

Soul of Cancers

I'm a **Cancer**, I'll always remember how you hurt me and the exact feeling I felt. Sometimes I'm too forgiving, sometimes I hold a grudge so intense you no longer exist in my memory.

Soul of Cancers

The past is a sensitive place for us **Cancers** because we never accept, we need to let go. We gate to go back on our promises even if we weren't at fault, we still find ways to blame ourselves and end up hurt. We hold those demons thinking we can turn them into something beautiful.

Soul of Cancers

Cancers *compatible* signs:

Pisces and **Scorpio**

Cancers opposite sign:

Capricorn

Cancers least compatible signs:

Aquarius, **Sagittarius**, **Leo**

Soul of Cancers

Which *signs* are you **most compatible**?

1.
2.
3.
4.

Which *signs* are not **least compatible**?

1.
2.
3.
4.

Which *sign* was the **most toxic**?

1.
2.
3.
4.

Which *signs* made the **best friends**?

1.
2.
3.
4.

Soul of Cancers

Compatibility:

Cancers and **Cancer**: the two of you are caring individuals and can understand each other at a depth no one can feel you. You are aware of the needs of each other and can attend to those needs, this can create a foundation for an undeniable connection. It can get a bit rocky when it comes to those overly sensitive moments, and you're both at a loss at how to help each other. You can space and feel the need to fix everything, so no pain is involved. Ghosting comes in handy when the confrontation comes to play because as Cancers we fear rejection. If the communication is there, this can be a connection worth it all. It's important to build that solid foundation.

Cancer and **Scorpio**: the two of you can provide each other a strong bond, but you need to be on the same page. Both Cancer and Scorpio are caring, emotional, and sensitive. Both have incredibly different ways of showing their love. Scorpios tend to demand more attention than they give, once they get comfortable and, in their element, they can be quite possessive. This is a complicated connection, if Scorpio can control their need to dominate the relationship, it will be a lot healthier. Scorpio is driven by sexual desires, as Cancer needs more than a physical connection. In many ways, you both can learn from each other and put the balance in your differences. Be aware that you will always be the one offering more of your love and affection openly, and you will be the calm to their storm every time.

Cancer and **Pisces**: you both are related by water; in this way, you hold a strong connection. You both are sensitive and emotional, and intuitive. Both of you share a psychic connection, sometimes you need to read each other's minds. Pisces are big dreamers and have many fantasies, and Cancer is someone who fits perfectly, they're nurturing and ready to offer reassurance. The two of you share a rare understanding in all aspects of life, but also the similarities between the two of you can get the best of you, it'd important to keep the balance and keep the communication going.

Soul of Cancers

Cancer and **Taurus**: the strongest part of this connection is the emotional security and how it's important to both of you, you bring it to the table, as does Taurus. You both love to show your affection and are amazing support systems to each other. Sexual excitement is high. Taurus is more cautious, Cancer is nurturing. Each of you compliments each other well if you don't lose the balance that keeps you both secure.

Cancer and **Gemini**: despite the differences each of you holds, there is a great potential for this connection to be a long-lasting one. Gemini has a realistic approach to life as you reply deeply to emotions and your intuition to guide you. Gemini will bring the extrovert out of you. Gemini is also the one to be the least stable and needs a partner that can balance them out and bring steady support because they seemed to get caught up in their emotions. The differences between the two of you will either make you stronger or break the bond altogether.

Cancer and **Leo**: You both are receptive to romance, on a passionate level, you will be a great pairing. Leo is vibrant, where you lack

Soul of Cancers

confidence, Leo will offer support. Your loving nature is appealing to Leo, but for any connection to work between the two of you, Leo will need to dim their energy a bit to understand you on a deeper level. As for us Cancers are timid and love to stay in our shells, this is the only dealbreaker for a relationship between you two. Leo tends to be too much and demanding too much from a Cancer when they're not ready or unable to fulfill will go nowhere.

Cancer and **Aries**: The only way for this relationship to work on a romantic level would be for Cancer to be the homemaker and Aries to be in control of the money. Aries love to take control and be the "boss" while Cancer is more laidback and needs constant reassurance when it comes to love and emotional stability. Aries are more independent and bossier, they're also resentful if they don't happen to get what they want. For this to work, Aries will need to have extra patience because Cancers are always willing to be there giving it another shot. There needs to be an emotional connection or there will be an emotional strain.

Soul of Cancers

Cancer and **Virgo**: Virgos are practical as Cancers are not. Your emotional nature allows you to be more behind your emotional and not practical side. There is any misunderstanding between the two of you which could lack the connection that you behold. Virgos can be difficult to please and it can be hard for them to handle your emotional changes. It's not easy for you to handle any kind of judgment but you're overly sensitive and Virgo doesn't comprehend that. You both are compatible when it comes to romance but there will be many hitches, so be aware of the signs.

Cancers and **Libra**: there is great intimacy between this connection, you both are bound to grow, and both of your signs are connected by the cardinal. Your emotional beings match, and with the outgoing Libra, they are often helping you to leave your shell from time to time. Libras tend to get bored easily, so you need to constantly keep the fire between the two of you, but don't let it be one-sided. Libra is also materialistic, and you also need money for a sense of security. The one issue between the two of you is you're more comfortable in a loving setting as Libra is someone that loves to go out and have fun. The energy isn't always matched.

Cancer and **Sagittarius**: water and fire, a questionable combination between the two of you. Sagittarius is more about going out and having fun, while you are content with staying out the party life. Sagittarius does not take things seriously, they find humor in just about everything. This relationship between the two of you will not be ideal, Sagittarius may be too blunt and may criticize too much, as Cancer could take this as a dealbreaker.

Cancer and **Capricorn**: people may think that being opposites attract, but you are likely to be drained by Capricorns because they consider any type of sensitiveness to weakness. They're cold-blooded. The reason Cancer is so attracted to Capricorn is because they try to find it in them to soften them. For you two to see eye to eye on any level, there needs to be a compromise. Many differences will hold this partnership back. You're not materialistic as Capricorn is. Capricorn is not that supportive. They're sweet talkers and are great at faking. This partnership can either be disastrous or work out.

Cancer and **Aquarius**: Aquarius is not someone who is in touch with their emotions, they choose thought and be practical. You're someone who is ruled by the moon, so emotions and being sensitive is nurturing to you. You're not very adventurous, it depends on the adventure, which can also be a turn-off for you. For this partnership to work you will need to find a middle ground. You both can create beautiful things, just might not be together.

Section:

"The Feels"

Soul of Cancers

I'm an **empath**, I feel too much of everyone. When I love them, their troubles become mine too. I try to heal them from their trauma. It's my love language, that's why it's important to release you if you're not bettering yourself. It's not love if I lose myself loving you.

Soul of Cancers

Emotional and intense, two traits I was never accepted for. I was always told to dim my emotions, that my love was too intense. It was too much, but they also wanted my love. It goes to show I've always been real; they were just not ready for my love.

Soul of Cancers

One reoccurring problem I have is **forgiving so easily**, letting people back into my life after I cut them out. I love hard, sometimes too hard it hurts to let go when I invested so much love. I've always been terrible at letting go even when I should have.

Soul of Cancers

My **vulnerability** isn't a weakness, it's a strength. I refuse to believe I'm weak because I opened my heart just for it to be damaged. I take pride in my vulnerable heart and the intensity it provides. I never gave mediocre love, even when it hurts, I always gave my all.

Soul of Cancers

I'm a "**look at the moon**" kind of person but I'm more of a "let me go find the moon" every time I know it's going to visit. I love the moon no matter what phase it's in. I love how alive I am when it's out. It takes all my energy but gives me endless peaceful vibes.

Soul of Cancers

I mastered the art of being known but no one truly knows. I like to keep a lot private, let people assume they do. It shows who's lives they care about more and where they need to invest energy.

Soul of Cancers

My love hits different. It's real. It's honest. It may overwhelm you but it's never going to hurt you.

Soul of Cancers

I don't read the room; **I can feel the room** and sometimes it's too much to handle. It's a lot of energy taken from me. Other's emotions affect me. it's my nature to try and save, heal, and love the broken. It hits too close to home for me. I just want my love to be cherished.

Soul of Cancers

I'm not big on opening to just anyone, letting them see me **vulnerable**. Not everyone gets to see that side of me because when you're open, you're not just open to love but you're open to pain. They seem to be equal the same in the end.

Soul of Cancers

My **loyalty** runs deep like my love. I would never hurt anyone I hold close to my heart. If you give me no choice and continue to take my kindness for weakness to see how long I'll stay, don't say it was me who broke us just because I had the courage to walk away.

I remember energy and vibes. I'm an observer, I pay attention to detail. I remember everything about someone I love in any form. I don't take what they say or do lightly, they deserve to have all of me, and I mean that without taking away from myself to do so.

Soul of Cancers

I wasn't a need; I was only desired when convenient. I was wanted but not wholeheartedly, my **big heart** put those to shame, so they chose to use my heart as a weapon against me. I always lost the game.

Soul of Cancers

My heart is big, but not big enough to be a convenience. My love doesn't deserve to be taken for less than it's worth.

Soul of Cancers

I let go of people
I wanted to keep around forever,
to me,
that's become my biggest strength.
If you know me,
you know my heart's big
and my love is unconditional.
If I let you go
it was for reasons
that doesn't need an explanation.
Other than it wasn't me,
it was you.

Soul of Cancers

If you push me away,
I promise you,
you won't find me where you left me.
My heart's big
but not big enough to deal with people
who decide to love me
when it's convenient for them.

Soul of Cancers

I let souls back in too many times the word sorry lost meaning. I gave directions to my heart after being hurt too many times. I didn't know telling someone how to love me wouldn't make them love me. I was creating my **heartbreak**.

Soul of Cancers

My **savior complex** was my red flag. I always believed my love could heal anyone, oh was I wrong.

Soul of Cancers

I went to the **past** many times trying to rewrite history, to create a new storyline. All I received was the same repeated narrative, I stopped looking for comfort behind doors that were already closed.

Soul of Cancers

No one will love you as I do, there's something authentic about it but that doesn't mean it was for you or wasn't toxic. My love only goes as far as it's reciprocated. I have this habit of holding on when I need to let go, to better myself, to grow.

Soul of Cancers

I don't blame my heart for the souls it never kept. I don't hold myself at regret for not being kept. I hold myself accountable for all my mistakes but never the flaws. I taught myself to always fight for what's love, what's right, never what I blinded myself to believe.

Soul of Cancers

I witnessed the dishonestly, unhealed, and unhealthy love. It taught my heart to never love the way I was loved, to always love more, always.

Soul of Cancers

It was hard to be loved, to be felt. My love was too intense for some. I was too sensitive, vulnerable, and amiable. I felt too much of everyone. I love intuitively. Incredibly bittersweet it was, to be an **empath**.

Soul of Cancers

Often, we go back to the past or something similar because of the feeling we once felt in hopes to feel it again. It's not just a love interest, this can be anything that once made you feel some source of comfort.

This can be a friend, or not even someone but something. It can be your favorite snack that was discontinued and came back with a new formula. It can be your favorite TV show coming back with a reboot.

We set expectations based on how they made us feel when we first witnessed, that's why we're disappointed when we realize they're not what we're used to. Things change, it's inevitable.

We need to understand nothing will ever be the same as we once felt, that's the beauty of memories they always remind you how something or someone made you feel, but sometimes that's the only time you'll feel it ever again and you need to make peace with that.

Soul of Cancers

I've never half loved anyone; I have always loved them with my whole heart. That's why they never deserved me because I don't know what it's like to give only a part of me, I always gave more than I should have.

Soul of Cancers

Nothing good came from me searching.
Nothing good came from me chasing. Every
time I searched and chased for love it was
always conditional, it was always one-sided.
When I focused on myself and finding
peace, my blessings slowly appeared.
Nothing good came from forcing.

Soul of Cancers

Outgrowing some people, some things have been the best thing to happen to my soul. Pain isn't as bad when it teaches you. Love isn't something you kill for, especially if it's taking the love away from you.

You outgrow people in your life when you outgrow what's holding you together. When you outgrow the pattern of behavior tied to trying to fight to keep you together. You outgrow people when you realize you can't make them grow with you.

You outgrow people who don't make it to see your growth up close when you outgrow the need to keep them around only because you love them.

You outgrow the facade of what you knew love to be when you felt what it wasn't. You outgrow the feeling of love you chased when you never got to feel it.

I outgrew the definition of love I fought so hard to feel when I loved many times, and they all were a different feel. I outgrew the idea I had of love when I didn't let what it didn't change me, but instead, help me grow. I outgrew every version of me when I let go of everything and everyone who wasn't healthily serving me. I outgrew the idea of holding onto forever when I accepted to live within the moment.

Soul of Cancers

Everyone in your life doesn't have a permanent stay, their intentions are always based on their conditions.

Soul of Cancers

You will only disturb your inner peace
checking in on those who brought you pain.
Close that door already.

Soul of Cancers

Soul of Cancers

Thank you for reading. I hope you felt a piece of you within each page. I hope you find comfort in my words and come back when you need some inspiration.

You are never alone, your emotional depth may be too much for some, but you're worthy and deserving.

Soul of Cancers

All platforms:

Twitter: @bymoonsoulchild
@soulofcancers

Instagram: @moonsoulchild
@soulofcancers

Tiktok: @bymoonsoulchild
@soulofcancers

Website: Moonsoulchild.com

Soul of Cancers

Printed in Great Britain
by Amazon